Oceans And Sunsets

A Collection of Love and Pain

Tanya L. Peters

BookLeaf Publishing

India | USA | UK

Made with ❤ on the BookLeaf Publishing Platform
www.bookleafpub.in
www.bookleafpub.com

Dedication

To Stacy...I promised.

And to my daughters, the loves of my life, Nevaeh and
Daelyn, I am who I am for you and because of you.
I love you so so much!

Preface

May these words meet your heart with a piercing compassion as a reminder that you are never alone. Whether in the depths of the ocean's waves or lost in the brilliance of the setting sun. Love is the affliction and the liberator.

Acknowledgements

Whether you have loved deeply, mourned profoundly, or simply stood in awe of life's fleeting beauty, this collection will speak to the depths of your heart. I'd like to acknowledge those who have loved me and those who have lost me along the way.

Aloneness

quiet severs reality
lathered in sharp brisk air
a sunken pit inside
overwhelmed with despair
a frail and shallow yearning
a touch a voice a sound
an empty heart thumps softly
no one else around

Mother

the moment I saw your face, so precious
My Heart
the moment you first said my name, so joyous
My Heart
the moment you hugged me and kissed my cheek, so
fulfilling
My Heart
the moment you met each milestone, so proud
My Heart
the moment you overcame the pain, so strong
My Heart
each moment you conquer this world, so powerful
My Heart

Been Here So Many Times

There's a darkness in the distance
Shades of black and gray
Approach it slow and mindful
Cannot go another way
The raindrops splatter one by one
Each one filled with so much pain
Stay focused while you navigate
Familiar with the rain
Soon the darkness fades away
Once again no blur just lines
New strength is an addition
Been here so many times

Exquisite Things

You are made of many facets
There's a sparkle in your eyes
The things you touch they shimmer
Your laughter grand in size
Your smile shines a spotlight
There's no darkness when you're there
The joy that's spread inside your words
Will make one stop and stare
Each step you take a symphony
With each breath the wind it sings
You are absolutely singular
Made of all exquisite things

Matchbox

Take me out of here
Light me on fire before you go
Free me from myself

Widow

The morning that you left me, my world was ripped
apart
My vision blurred, my voice no sound, my chest a
bleeding heart
Time spins around me endlessly, the darkness overcomes
Mind searching for the memories, of lost times that were
once
We were, we had, we used to be, we everything past
tense
Now what we were supposed to be is gone it makes no
sense
Who will love me now, who will know me like you do
Who will keep my secrets, and who will know what's
true
Who will make more memories, who will laugh with me
Who will be there when I'm scared, I just need you to be
Who will help me raise our girls, who will hold us tight
Who will I rest my head upon when I awake at night
Who'll accept me as I am, and when I'm blind who'll be
my sight

Who'll take those trips we talked about, by land and sea
and flight
Who will I grow old with, who will I walk beside
Who will shield me from the rain, where will I go to hide
I just can't figure out what it is I'm going to do
I never dreamed I'd live this life not side by side with you
You've always been my comfort zone, in chaos you were
clear
And now that life is upsidedown, there's no ease to my
fear
I wish, I want, I hope you knew, if only there could be
Why can't, why not, where are you now, why aren't you
here with me
They say that ease will find my pain, that light will fill
my soul,
But what they will not ever know is that my world, it
won't be whole
They'll never know a love like ours, they'll never feel this
pain
They'll never just what I've lost, it's not simple and plain
They'll never know what's deep inside, when they look
into my eyes
They'll never know my broken soul, they'll never hear
my cries
You see, my love, you took with you not just a piece of
me
You left me with my mangled heart, exposed for all to

see

No way that I can cover up, no bandage for my sorrow
No love, no hope, no happiness, no promise of tomorrow

Delusion

Hands so gentle
Holding my heart
Gifts of pleasure
And tearing apart

Goodbye

heart of wax
warmed by touch
delicate hold
not too tight
begins to melt
tightened grasp
puddle of memories

Breathe

His touch sets me on fire
Hands slide up and down my spine
His inferno brands my skin
As he whispers this is mine
He pulls me close to breathe my breath
A quiet moan escapes
His fingers circle over me
As my body's motion shapes
He lays me back and spreads my thighs
He's built up a gentle force
I submit to him so easily
So steady no remorse
He gathers me within his hands
He watches as I fall
Our breath out of control now
His name a quiet call
Attentively he activates
He takes me to my peak
Selflessly he handles me
His motion makes me weak

I reach for him to pull him close
Demanding what I need
His thrust returns me to my place
His strength to plant his seed
I can't hold back I've reached the end
I scream he's hit my limit
We hold onto each other
Then take a moment to begin it

I Am The Magic

I'm the vibrance of the sunset
You can't believe your eyes are seeing
I'm the waves that crash up on the sand
That justify your being
I'm the reason you know what love is
Because I'm branded on your soul
I'm the ache you feel deep in your chest
That tells you you're not whole
I'm that joyful tune that when you hear
It always makes you smile
I'm at the depths of your tired sigh
That lets you know life's worthwhile
It's me that's there when you feel that breeze
That sweeps across your face
It's me there in the darkness too
When you reach for that embrace
I'm the moment that it dawns on you
That maybe you were wrong
I'm the only memory of love
That you've known all along

I'm the pit inside your stomach
Cause you know that this is tragic
Cause you walked away and let me go
And now you know I am the magic

Always Us

Like the ocean and the
Sand together
Through waves of life we can
Stand together
Separated by time too many times
Always trust
Cause 'til the end of time it's
Always us

Sinking

I call out to you in my dreams
I wonder where you are
I'm sinking here without you
Life's taken you too far

Colors

Your love feels like a sunset
Glowing pink purple and blue
Across white caps of the ocean
Where I can never quite reach you
It fills my eyes with colored tears
That burn my mind and soul
And make me feel this fleeting moment
Is out of my control
The light breeze against my cheeks
Carries salted air into my chest
And the sand beneath my feet
So soft yet sturdy so I rest

Fear of Love

Come to me my love
Bring your heart close
Don't be afraid
Place it in my hands
Soft and gentle
I will protect it
I will hold on tight
Release your fears
And extend your hands
Steady and calm
Unwavering and strong
And I will place my heart with you

Knots

Dawn has arrived it's time to go
Make sure you're breathing deep
Keep your feet planted and your spine straight
Time's past you were asleep
Look forward now but don't forget
The steps are here and now
Keep the tools you've gathered up
Fill your cup and then allow
It's ok to stumble on your way
Take the chance and then repeat
Squeeze out every lesson
There's no victory in retreat
No one brings what you can bring
Use every moment time allots
The strength is in the journey
So keep your laces tied in knots

Fingerprints

I remember when you promised
Said you'd protect me from the world
Said you'd be right by my side
When this life's chaos unfurled
The love I felt etched on my heart
Spills like waterfalls of blood
Evasive love that tore me down
Reaching dragging through the mud
Tried and tried without success
To open up your eyes
Each time open and empty
Deciphering your lies
Picked me up began to see
Had to sew my heart back up
I see you now don't feel a thing
Looking past you with a stare
Erased you from my memory
But your fingerprints still there

Heartache

Lost in a desert of loneliness
Thirsty for a drop of intimacy
Locked up in the darkness
A prison of solitude
Lost at sea in isolation
Yearning to be loved
Gasping for air
Atop a mountain
Heart trying to breathe

Smile

I woke up today and put a smile on
I wear it every day
I do all the tasks they ask of me
I put all the sad away
It's how I live my life these days
Just trying to be strong
I close my eyes and think of you
And how it's been so long
I remember every inch of you
Every look upon your face
I still pick up my phone to call
It's like I feel a trace
Your spirit lives inside of me
And inside both our girls
I see you in their faces
In their laughs and in their curls
I talk I know you hear me
I wish you could be here
I know you're waiting there for me
And in that I never fear

So while you're on my mind today
As I'm fighting back the pain
I want to say I Love You
Now until we meet again

Washed Away

I was the ocean
You stayed in the rivers
I was the universe
You only saw stars
I was the mountain
You stood safe in the valley
I was the sun
You searched for the shade
I was the life
You afraid to live
I was the love
You remained in your pain
I was the ocean
And I washed you away

I Remember

It's so strange the moving on
One day you've forgotten
And the next engulfed in emotions
Sometimes I don't want you to visit my mind
And sometimes I smile when I think of you
Sometimes I smile and hold you in my dreams
Other times I scream out for you
But you never turn around
There are days that the breath leaves my lungs
And the pain is crippling
Each time I laugh
I look for you to share my joy
When I'm scared I remember how it felt
To be shielded by your protection
On the days when I feel most alone
I dig down to where I keep you now
I open the door and let myself feel
A little taste of the love that you left with me
It burns a bit but a sweet sensation
Elated knowing it's only mine to have

Not another soul on this earth has this piece of you
You loved no one else like this
It's mine to keep forever
Tucked away
I miss you
I remember

Wrong Side of Midnight

It's inevitable, this thing between you and me
The universe conspires, placing us together like two and
three
We think we make our ways, digging our grooves in two
directions
But the pull takes over us making just one out of two
reflections
We defy the creator of this life and all it manifests to be
in control
But we are weakened by its power shifting time and
space to make two halves one whole
We are intertwined in our thoughts and our bodies are
magnets in small spaces
We tell ourselves we are where we belong but the
tragedy reads all over our faces
And when the days lay to rest and the speak our names
so bright
We ache longing for each other from the wrong side of
midnight